Plant Growth and Development

STUDENT ACTIVITY BOOK

SCIENCE AND TECHNOLOGY FOR CHILDREN

NATIONAL SCIENCE RESOURCES CENTER
Smithsonian Institution–National Academy of Sciences
Arts and Industries Building, Room 1201
Washington, DC 20560

NSRC

The National Science Resources Center is operated by the National Academy of Sciences and the Smithsonian Institution to improve the teaching of science in the nation's schools. The NSRC collects and disseminates information about exemplary teaching resources, develops and disseminates curriculum materials, and sponsors outreach activities, specifically in the areas of leadership development and technical assistance, to help school districts develop and sustain hands-on science programs. The NSRC is located in the Arts and Industries Building of the Smithsonian Institution and in the Capital Gallery Building in Washington, D.C.

ISBN 0-89278-634-5

Published by Carolina Biological Supply Company, 2700 York Road, Burlington, NC 27215.
Call toll free 800-334-5551.

CB787059607

Contents

Fast Plants for Fast Times

The Wisconsin Fast Plant™ is the plant you will be using for your experiments in this unit. It took Dr. Paul Williams, who is a professor and researcher at the University of Wisconsin, about 15 years to develop it. Fifteen years may seem like a very long time to spend breeding a plant, but think of all that he accomplished. Through selective breeding, Dr. Williams was able to speed up the plant's life cycle, making it ten times faster than that of its ancestors. Today, this small, yellow-flowered plant whizzes through its entire life cycle, from seed to seed, in just 6 weeks.

Dr. Williams had an interesting reason for wanting to develop a fast plant. He is a plant pathologist, and his job is to study plant diseases and to find out if some plants inherit the ability to fight off diseases. In order to speed up his work, he needed a fast-growing plant to use in his studies.

Dr. Williams started with a world collection of more than 2,000 *Brassica* seeds and planted them in his laboratory using planting, lighting, and watering equipment almost exactly like what you will use. He observed that out of the 2,000, only a few plants flowered much sooner than others. He took advantage of these exceptional plants by cross-breeding them. These few would be the parents of his next generation of plants. Dr. Williams wondered what kind of offspring these faster flowering parents would produce. Would the offspring inherit the ability to flower earlier than the average *Brassica* plant?

Yes! In fact, a few of the new plants even flowered a little faster than the parent plants. These slightly faster offspring were then cross-pollinated, becoming the parents of the next generation.

Dr. Williams continued to use this method of selective breeding for years. He grew

populations of 288 or more plants in each generation. He cross-bred the earliest flowering plants of this population and used their seeds to grow the next generation. In each new generation, he found that about 10 percent of the plants flowered slightly earlier than their parent generation had.

The selective breeding project was a grand success. The result is what is now known as Wisconsin Fast Plants™. Besides developing a 6-week growth cycle, Dr. Williams was able to breed in other desirable qualities that make the plant a nearly ideal laboratory tool. Some outstanding traits of these plants are:

- They produce lots of pollen and eggs, resulting in many fertile seeds.

- Their seeds do not need a dormancy (or rest) period, so they can be replanted immediately.

- The plants are small and compact.

- They thrive in a crowd.

- They grow well under constant light.

Wisconsin Fast Plants have become important laboratory research tools all over the world. Soon they will be part of National Aeronautics and Space Administration's space biology program. But most exciting of all, these special plants are becoming part of school science programs across the country, from the elementary to the university level.

| LESSON 1 | # What Do You Know about Plants? |

Think and Wonder

Plants are all around us. You probably know many things about plants already. During this unit, you will have a chance to learn a lot more. What do you know about plants? What would you like to learn?

Materials

For you
    1 dry lima bean seed
    1 student notebook
    1 **Activity Sheet 1, Recording Chart for Seed Observations**

For you and your partner
    1 hand lens

Find Out for Yourself

1. Take out your student notebook and put your name in it. You will use your notebook during this unit to record ideas and observations and to store the activity sheets you will use.

2. Now you are ready to start thinking about plants. What would you like to learn about plants? Raise your hand when you have something to add. Your teacher will keep a list of everyone's ideas. There is a special name for discussing ideas together as a class. It is called brainstorming. Your teacher has probably told you some rules to follow when brainstorming.

3. After you have finished discussing plants, you have a second task: looking at seeds with a hands lens. Your teacher will show you how to pick up the seed and the hand lens. Figure 1-1 shows you how.

4. Use your hand lens to *look* at the seed. Observe its color and shape. Record your findings on the activity sheet.

5. *Touch* the seed. It is dry. What other words can you use to tell how the seed feels? Write those words beside the heading "Texture" on your Activity Sheet.

Figure 1-1

Using a hand lens

6. *Smell* the seed. Does it have an odor? Record your findings.

7. How big is your dry seed? Lay it on a ruler to measure it or trace around it.

8. Be sure to record all of your seed observations on **Activity Sheet 1**, the recording chart. Keep the chart in your student notebook.

9. Clean up. Return the hand lens to where you got it. For the last part of the lesson, drop your dry bean seed into the container of water your teacher has set out.

10. What do you think will happen to the bean seed soaking in water overnight? Why? Share your ideas with the class and your teacher, who will write them down on the board. They are called predictions.

Ideas to Explore

1. Do a seed survey at home. How many different kinds of seeds and seed products can you find? Keep a list.

2. Bring in seeds to share with your classmates. Put them in the learning center in your classroom. Look in your lunch for seeds. You may see seeds hiding in apples and other fruits. Look on the playground for seeds, too.

3. Do you know any seed songs? Share them with the class.

What Is Inside a Seed?

Think and Wonder

Have you ever thought about what a seed looks like inside? It has tiny parts. If you look closely, you can see how they are different. What does each part do? Why are they important?

Materials

For you

1 **Activity Sheet 1, Recording Chart for Seed Observations**
2 to 3 soaked lima bean seeds
1 dry lima bean seed
1 paper towel
1 student notebook

For you and your partner

1 hand lens

Find Out for Yourself

1. First, let's review. How many of these questions can you answer?

   ■ What are the five senses?

   ■ What did you observe about the dry bean?

   ■ What did you predict would happen to the seed when it was soaked in water overnight?

2. Now, pick up your supplies. Look at the outside of the soaked bean seed. Notice how the seed coat has changed. Find the seed scar, the place where the seed used to be attached to the parent plant. Describe the seed using as many of your senses as possible. But remember, no tasting. Measure your wet seed the same way you measured the dry seed. Is there any difference?

3. Record this information on **Activity Sheet 1.**

4. Next, peel off the seed coat and pry the seed open. Look inside the seed. Be very gentle.

5. Use your hand lens to observe the inside of the bean seed. Find the baby plant, which is also called the embryo. The rest of the seed is food for the embryo.

6. Look at the embryo very carefully. Find the parts that you think will become:

   ■ the roots

   ■ the stem

   ■ the leaves

7. Your teacher will pass out extra bean seeds. Observe your extra bean seeds in exactly the same way. If you're careful, you should find the same parts in each one.

8. Now you are ready to make a scientific drawing. Draw the inside of your bean seed. Be sure to make it big enough so that you can see all the parts clearly.

9. Draw a straight line to the embryo and write its name as a label. Then draw a straight line to the food supply and write its name as a label.

   Here is an example of a scientific drawing with labels.

Figure 2-1

Scientific drawing

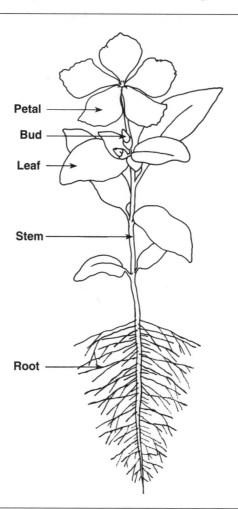

Petal

Bud

Leaf

Stem

Root

10. Clean up. Place your Activity Sheet in your notebook. Wrap the seeds in the paper towel and throw them away. Return the hand lens to its container.

Ideas to Explore

1. Look inside other seeds for embryos. Peanuts are good ones to look at.

Figure 2-2

Peanuts

2. Find out why a baby plant needs to have a good food supply along with it while it is underground.

3. You observed the seed scar today. It marks the place where the seed used to be attached to the parent plant while it was still in the pod. Where is your "seed scar"? What do you call it?

LESSON 3	# Planting the Seed

Think and Wonder

Have you ever worked in a garden? If you have, you know you must be careful how you put seeds in the ground. During this lesson, you will be planting seeds that grow very fast. Read how to plant them on the instruction sheet that your teacher will give to you.

Materials

For you

1	student notebook
1	tray
1	planter quad
1	cup of soil
12	fertilizer pellets
1	toothpick
1	pair of forceps
1	spoon
4	wicks
8	seeds
1	planter label
1	paper towel
1	**Activity Sheet 2, How to Plant Wisconsin Fast Plants™ Seeds**

For you and your partner

1	pair of forceps
1	cup of water and dropper

Find Out for Yourself

1. Pick up your supplies. Then your teacher will hand out a copy of **Activity Sheet 2**. Read the directions on the sheet to help you plant the seeds correctly.

2. Plant your seeds, following the directions very carefully. If you don't understand something, ask your teacher or a classmate.

3. When you have finished planting, return all leftover supplies to the distribution station.

4. **Clean up your work space**. Do your fair share.

5. Think back about what you learned about seeds in Lessons 1 and 2. What happened to seeds that were soaked? Make a prediction about what will happen to the seeds you planted today. Write your predictions in your notebook.

Ideas to Explore

Plant a variety of other seeds and compare their growth to the Wisconsin Fast Plants™.

LESSON 4	# Thinning and Transplanting

Think and Wonder

Have you ever worked in a garden? If so, you may have noticed that some plants are stronger than others. To help the stronger ones grow even better, you have to pull out the weak ones. This process is called thinning. In this lesson, you will thin your plants. Then you can transplant the extra ones to another planter.

Materials

For you
1 toothpick
1 student notebook

For you and your partner
1 hand lens
1 pair of forceps or scissors (optional)

Find Out for Yourself

1. One of your gardening activities will be thinning out the seedlings. Discuss why you think it might be a good idea for only one plant to live in each planter section.

2. Another important task you will be doing today is transplanting. Transplanting means gently digging up a plant, roots and all, and replanting it in another place. Be ready to give two reasons why transplanting is a good idea.

3. Now you are ready to begin working with your plants. First, pick up your plants from under the lights. Then, observe them with a hand lens. Do they all look the same?

4. Count your plants. Did all eight of your seeds sprout, or germinate?

5. Next, decide which one plant from each section you will keep and which ones you will thin out. You should have a total of four plants in your planter, one per section.

6. Use a toothpick to loosen the potting mix in your planter quad. Then use the forceps to uproot one of your extra seedlings. Put it aside to observe and draw later.

7. Thin until you have one plant per section (Figure 4-1, A). You have a choice of two ways to thin:

   ■ Cut off the extra seedlings close to the potting mix. You may use your fingers or scissors.

   ■ Loosen the potting mix with a toothpick. Uproot the extra seedlings with forceps.

Figure 4-1

Thinning and transplanting seedlings

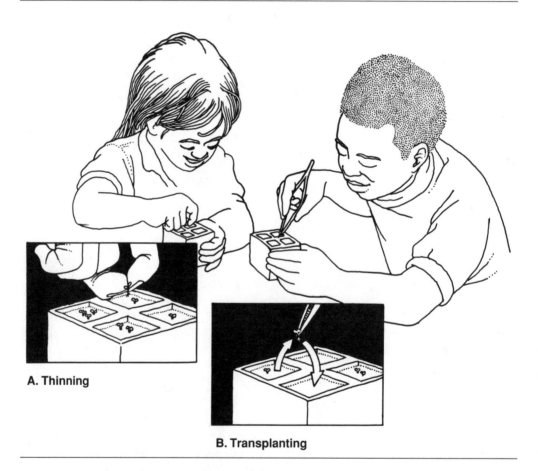

A. Thinning

B. Transplanting

---

8. If you have uprooted the seedlings, decide where you want to put them. You have three choices:

   ■ Transplant them into one of your own empty planter sections where no seeds germinated (Figure 4-1, B)

   ■ Donate them to a classmate for transplanting

   ■ Transplant them in a container your teacher has prepared

9. To transplant, poke a hole about 2 centimeters deep (your whole pencil point up to the paint) in the potting mix of the container you have chosen.

10. Using forceps, gently place the seedling in the hole. Press down the soil a little.

11. In your science notebook, record your observations of the seedling you put aside. First, draw and label the uprooted seedling. Include all of these parts in your drawing:

   ■ the seed leaves

   ■ the stem

   ■ the roots

12. Write about the seedling you drew. Describe the colors you observed in the different parts of the plant.

13. Finally, don't forget to write today's date and the age of your seedling on the observation page.

14. Clean up thoroughly. Put the equipment back. Throw away trash.

Ideas to Explore

1. What do you think would happen to your plants if you did not thin them out?

2. Imagine that you are a plant living alone, in a small planter. There is enough air, food, water, light, and soil to make life very easy. Suddenly three more seeds sprout, right in your planter. Now there are four of you! How will your life change? What kinds of problems will you have? How could the problems be solved? Write a short story about it in your notebook.

How Does Your Plant Grow?

Think and Wonder

How tall is your plant? How much has it grown since you planted it? During this lesson, you will learn easy ways to measure your plant and graph its progress.

Materials

For you

 1 quad of plants
 1 student notebook
 1 sheet of centimeter graph paper
 1 strip of graph paper cut 1 centimeter wide
 1 pair of scissors
 1 ruler marked in centimeters (optional)
   Snap-together centimeter cubes (optional)
   Glue

Find Out for Yourself

1. Your teacher will give you a piece of graph paper. Use it to keep a record of how much your plant grows from day to day. Be sure to record the date and the age of your plant each time you measure.

2. Pick out the one plant that you will measure during the unit. Move your name label into that plant's section of the planter. Now you have a marker to tell you which plant to measure each time.

3. There are two different ways to measure and graph: using paper strips and using snap-together centimeter cubes. Use one of these techniques. Here are instructions for measuring and graphing using paper strips.

   ■ Hold the paper strip behind the plant you are measuring. Be sure the bottom of the strip is touching the agreed upon spot (either the potting mix or the pot rim, whichever your class decided).

   ■ Draw a line on the strip to mark the height of your plant.

Figure 5-1

Measuring with paper strips

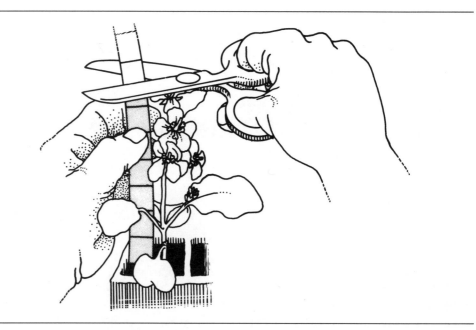

- Color in the squares that are below that line.

- Double-check that you measured correctly by holding the paper strip up against the plant again.

- Then, cut off the darkened squares as shown in Figure 5-1. Lay the darkened strip on your graph above the correct day number. Paste it neatly in place.

4. Here are instructions for measuring and graphing using the snap-together centimeter cubes.

- Snap together some cubes until you think you have enough to measure how tall your plant is. Make your best estimate.

- Hold your tower of cubes behind the plant, as shown in the illustration below. Make sure the bottom is resting on the agreed upon place (either the potting mix or the pot rim).

- Add or subtract cubes until your plant and the cubes match in height.

Figure 5-2

Using cubes to measure and graph

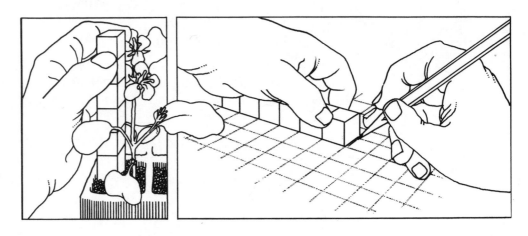

- Lay the cubes on your graph above the correct day number. Mark the height on the graph (Figure 5-2).

- Darken in the bar graph up to that height.

5. Give your graph a title. Place it in your notebook and add to it each day.

Ideas to Explore

1. Was everyone's plant exactly the same height when the class measured today? Why do you think the plants varied in size?

2. There are probably a lot of differences in height among your classmates, too. Why do you think this is true?

3. Practice measuring objects in the science center. How long is a paper clip? Is a bean seed the same length as the paper clip?

4. Practice measuring yourself in centimeters with a meter stick or tape measure. Measure your foot (from the big toe to the heel). Then measure your forearm (from the elbow to the wrist). Compare the two measurements. Are you surprised at the results?

| LESSON 6 | # Observing Leaves and Flower Buds |

Think and Wonder

As plants grow, not only do they get taller, but they also develop new parts. Your plant has grown big enough so you can see two kinds of leaves and flower buds. The directions below tell you what to look for in your growing plant and how to record your observations.

Materials

For you
    1 quad of plants with buds
    1 **Observation Sheet**
    1 student notebook

For you and your partner
    1 hand lens

Find Out for Yourself

1. Observe your plants with a hand lens. First, focus on the leaves. Look at them very closely. Count how many there are.

   The two heart-shaped leaves closest to the soil are the seed leaves. They were the first leaves to appear. The newer leaves, above the seed leaves, are called true leaves. Notice that the true leaves are very different from the seed leaves.

2. Next, focus on the buds. Notice their color and shape.

3. Record your observations on your **Observation Sheet**. Begin by drawing your plant. Label all its parts. Here are a few hints to help you do a good job on the drawing:

   ▪ Show the difference between the seed leaves and the true leaves in your picture.

   ▪ Put the buds in the right place.

   ▪ Count the leaves to make sure you draw the right number.

4. Next, write about your plant. Need some helpful hints? A few are listed below:

   ■ Describe how the two kinds of leaves are different.

   ■ Describe the size and shape of each kind of leaf.

   ■ Tell how the two kinds of leaves feel. But touch the leaves very carefully.

   ■ Describe the colors of the buds.

5. Don't forget to put the date on your **Observation Sheet** and write down the age of your plant. Place your **Observation Sheet** in your notebook.

Ideas to Explore

1. Do you ever eat leaves? Name some of your favorite leaves.

2. Have you ever eaten buds or flowers? Name some buds or flowers that people eat. (These may be hard to think of!)

3. Bring in some leaves or buds to add to the science center. Be sure to ask permission before you pick anything.

4. Dissect a large bud, such as magnolia, hollyhock, or brussels sprouts. Use forceps and toothpicks to peel away the layers. What do you see?

Observing the Growth Spurt

Think and Wonder

If you have an older brother or sister, you may have noticed that when they turn 12 or 13, they start to grow very fast. This period is called a growth spurt. Your plant has a growth spurt, too. It usually happens between 9 and 13 days after you planted the seed. During this lesson, you will have time to observe, measure, and record your plant's growth spurt.

As you work, try to make predictions about how much you think your plant will grow by the next day. A prediction is different from a wild guess. To make a good prediction, you need to start with observations, experiences, and scientific reasons. For instance, the weather forecaster bases predictions for tomorrow's weather on observations about the weather today and on measurements of temperature, wind direction, and air pressure.

Of course, like weather forecasters, even if your predictions are based on good information, you will not always be right! But with experience you will probably get better and better at making predictions.

Keep in mind that you don't know exactly when your plant will have its growth spurt. Not every plant is on the same timetable. That's why it's important to take measurements very often during the next week. If you can, take measurements every school day.

Materials

For you

1   quad of plants
1   sheet of centimeter graph paper
1   **Activity Sheet 3, Observing the Growth Spurt**
1   measuring strip or 1 set of centimeter cubes
1   pair of scissors
1   student notebook

Find Out for Yourself

1. Today you will begin keeping records of your plant's growth spurt. You will make observations, take measurements, and make predictions every school day for a week.

2. Your teacher will give you a recording chart—**Activity Sheet 3**—to keep in your notebook. Use it to record your plant's growth spurt.

3. In the column under the heading **Day**, write how many days it has been since you planted the seed. Under the heading **Today's Date**, write the date.

4. Observe your plant carefully. Write your observations in the correct space. Use as much space as you need.

5. Measure the height of your plant in centimeters. Then, measure it again to be sure you are right. Record the height in the column called **Height Today**.

6. Now, look at your plant and think about how much your plant will grow by tomorrow. This is your prediction. Cut a strip of paper or build a stack of centimeter cubes to show what your prediction is. Hold your prediction strip or stack up next to your plant. Ask yourself: "Is this how tall I think my plant will be tomorrow?" If the answer is yes, record your prediction.

7. Record your plant's height on your graph, too.

8. Clean up and place **Activity Sheet 3** and your graph back into your notebook.

9. At the end of the week, look at your data. Answer these questions using the information on your chart and graph:

   - On which days did your plant grow the most?

   - How tall was your plant before the growth spurt? How tall was it after the growth spurt?

   - How close were your predictions to what really happened?

Figure 7-1

Growth spurt

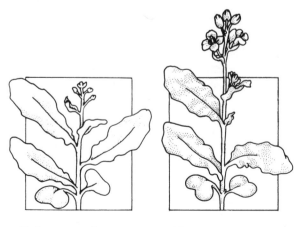

Before growth spurt   **After growth spurt**

**Ideas to
Explore**

Interview a parent or a relative about their growth spurt.

Figure 7-2

*"Look how
you've grown!"*

Why Are Bees Important?

Think and Wonder

In the spring and summer, we often see bees buzzing around flowers. Have you ever wondered why? During this lesson, you will have a chance to share what you already know about this interesting relationship in nature.

Materials

For you

1   sheet of drawing paper
    Crayons (optional)

Find Out for Yourself

1.   You probably know something about bees already, such as how they look and sound, what they eat and make, or where they live. Think of some of the things you know about bees that you would like to share with the class. Then think of some questions about bees that make you wonder.

2.   Your class discussion will be a brainstorming session much like the one you had during Lesson 1. Follow your teacher's rules like you did last time. The rules help make brainstorming fun for everyone.

Figure 8-1

Students brainstorming

3. After you have talked about bees, your teacher will give you art supplies. Use them to draw a bee. You may want to color the bee, too. Do the best job you can, but don't worry if your drawing is not perfect.

4. Give the drawing to your teacher to keep for you. At the end of the unit, when you are more of a bee expert, you will make another drawing. Then you will compare the two drawings to see what you have learned.

5. Why do you think bees are in this unit? How do you think bees are related to the *Brassica* plants you have been working with?

Ideas to Explore

Bees can be fascinating! Read to find out the answers to these questions:

- What is a "honey stomach"?

- Why do bees dance?

- Do the African bees deserve the name "killer bees"? Why or why not?

Getting a Handle on Your Bee

Think and Wonder

Have you ever looked at a bee up close? During this lesson, you will have a chance to observe its body parts. And you will make a bee stick by gluing the bee to a toothpick.

Materials

For you
- 1 dried bee
- 1 toothpick
- 1 tray
- 1 pair of forceps
- 1 **Activity Sheet 4, How to Make a Bee Stick**
- 1 hand lens

For every four students
- 1 cup
- 1 small cup of white glue

Find Out for Yourself

1. Your teacher will pass out **Activity Sheet 4**. It tells you how to make a bee stick. Read the directions with your class. Make sure you understand what to do.

2. Pick up your supplies. Follow the directions to make the bee stick. When you are done, your bee will have a "handle."

3. Take the time to really observe the bee closely. How many body parts can you find? (**Note:** Some bees may be damaged and not have all their parts. Ask a classmate to share if your bee is not complete.)

4. Push the bee stick into the bottom of an upside-down paper cup that your teacher put at your work space. Your teacher will store them in a safe place.

5. Clean up. Do your part to help.

6. Be ready to share some of your bee observations when your teacher projects the overhead transparency of the bee's body.

Ideas to Explore

1. Do some reading about bees and other insects.

2. Share with the class an insect collection that you might have at home.

3. Be on the lookout for other insects to observe. Notice what they have in common with bees. Notice how they are different.

Looking at Flowers

Think and Wonder

Have you ever looked closely at a flower? It has several tiny, delicate parts. Can you draw a *Brassica* flower?

Materials

For you
- 1 flowering plant
- 1 student notebook
- 1 **Observation Sheet**

For you and your partner
- 1 hand lens

Find Out for Yourself

1. Observe your plant. Use a hand lens to observe the flowers.

2. Share your observations with the class. What did you notice about the flower? Don't worry if you don't know the names of all the parts. Your teacher will help you learn the names of the important parts of the flower.

3. Draw and label in your notebook one of your *Brassica* flowers. Here are some ways to check your work:

    ■ Did you draw all the flower parts? Count to be sure.

    ■ Does each part appear to be the right size?

    ■ Is each part in the right place?

4. Read about the crucifer family on pg. 31 to find out more about your plant and its family.

5. Determine how many different crucifers from the list on pg. 32 you have tasted. Your teacher will ask you to raise your hand if you have tasted one of the crucifers.

Ideas to Explore

1. Are there any plants flowering in your neighborhood right now? Try taking one of them apart. Tape each flower part to a piece of paper and label it. Does it have the same parts as your *Brassica* flower? (**Note:** Be sure to ask permission before you pick any flower!)

2. The next time you are in the grocery store, go on a crucifer hunt. How many different crucifers can you find?

3. Do you know what part of the crucifer plant we eat? It may be a root, stem, leaves, or flowers. Look at the list on pg. 32. Which part of those plants do we eat?

Reading Selection

The Crucifer Family

It may seem odd to you that your plant belongs to a family, but it's true. Of course, it's not the kind of family with aunts and cousins and sisters. Think of it more as a group of plants that are alike in some ways.

Your *Brassica* plant belongs to the crucifer family. Crucifers have one thing in common. This feature gives the plants their family name. Here is a hint. The shape of their flowers is always like this:

Figure 10-1

Brassica *flowers*

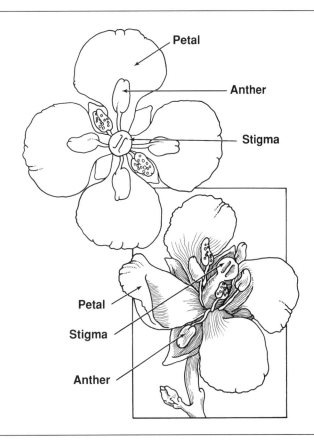

Did you figure out how the crucifer family got its name? The reason is that the crucifer flower always has four petals arranged in a cross. Scientists group all these flowers into the crucifer family.

A CRUCIFER SURVEY

The crucifers are an important food crop in many parts of the world. Which ones have you tasted?

Cabbage

Turnip

Collard

Watercress

Kohlrabi

Choy sum

Cauliflower

Broccoli

Rutabaga

Radish

Kale

Horseradish

Pak choi (Chinese mustard)

Brussels sprouts

Mustard greens

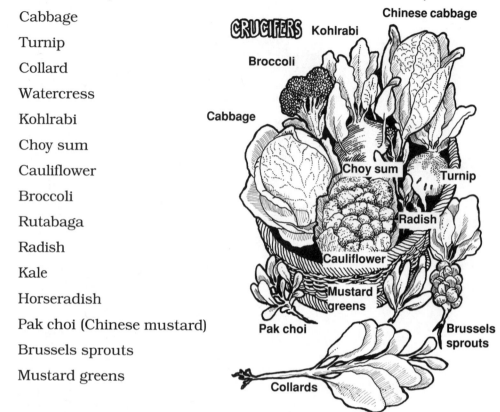

Some crucifer seeds are crushed for their oil. Others, like turnips, kale, and rutabagas, are good food for sheep and cattle as well as for people. Still others, like alyssum and candy tuft, are known for their beautiful flowers. There is even a branch of "bad guys" in the family, some pesky weeds!

Pollinating Flowers

Think and Wonder

From Day 13 to Day 18, you will cross-pollinate your plants. How are bees and flowers related? Why is cross-pollination important? Read more about this on pg. 35.

Materials

For you

   1 bee stick

      Plants with open flowers

For you and your partner

   1 hand lens

Find Out for Yourself

1. Pick up your materials.

2. For the next five days, pollinate every blossom that is open.

   Follow these directions:

   ■ Place your bee against a blossom and rotate the stick gently.

   ■ Move the bee to the blossom of *another plant*. Rotate gently.

   ■ Continue to "buzz" back and forth between the plants until all of the open blossoms have been pollinated. Work slowly, carefully, and gently.

3. Stop! Observe! Look for pollen on different parts of the flower. Look for pollen on the bee.

4. Clean up.

5. Be ready to share some of your observations about the bee and the flower when your teacher projects the overhead transparency called "Bee Pollinating a *Brassica* Flower."

6. Read *The Bee and the* Brassica: *Interdependence* on pg. 35.

Ideas to Explore

1. Try to learn more about pollination by reading or viewing a filmstrip or video.

2. On the day that you thinned your plants, you probably transplanted some of your extra plants into the class container. Today your teacher will put a sign on the container to remind you *not* to pollinate these plants. What do you predict will be the results of this experiment? How will the pollinated plants be different from the unpollinated plants? You'll find out by the end of the unit.

Reading Selection

The Bee and the *Brassica*: Interdependence

Bees and *Brassica* plants need each other in order to live. Each one takes something from the other and gives something in return. You might say that they have a real partnership.

Why does a flower need a bee? The main reason is so that the flower can make seeds. The *Brassica* flower holds both the male and the female parts of the plant. The male parts, the filament and anther, produce the pollen, which looks like fine yellow powder. Pollen must travel to the female parts, the pistil and stigma, of another flower on a different *Brassica* plant. Unless the pollen from one plant can reach another plant, no new seeds will form. Then, no new *Brassica* seedlings will grow.

Figure 11-1

Brassica *flower*

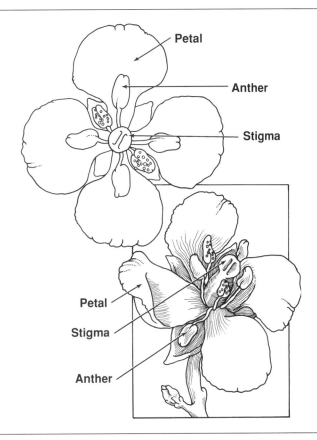

So it is very important that the pollen get from one plant to another. But the problem is that the pollen is sticky and cannot easily travel in the wind. How can the pollen travel? That's where the worker bee comes in. With its bright yellow color and sweet perfume, the flower lures the bee and offers not only one but two kinds of food: nectar and pollen.

The bee's body is covered with feathery hairs. As the bee dips her head into the flower to sip the sweet nectar deep inside the blossom, its hairy body rubs against the anthers holding the pollen. Her body traps some of it. When the bee flies off to the next flower, some of the pollen on her body sticks to the stigma there.

Now the bee has done her job. The bee has collected two kinds of food from the flower. At the same time, she has carried pollen from one flower to another. New seeds will form. Soon new flowers will bloom.

Figure 11-2

Bee pollinating a Brassica *flower*

LESSON 12	# Observing Pods

Think and Wonder

Between Day 17 and Day 35, your plant will be changing a lot. Pay special attention to the flowers. They are changing the most. What changes do you see?

Materials

For you

  1 plant with pods developing
  1 sheet of graph paper
  1 **Observation Sheet**
  1 toothpick (optional)
  1 student notebook

For you and your partner

  1 hand lens
  1 pair of forceps

Find Out for Yourself

1. Observe your plant. Use your hand lens to study the flowers. Are they still there?

2. What has happened to the petals? What about the anthers and the pistil? Be ready to share your observations.

Figure 12-1

Looking at pods

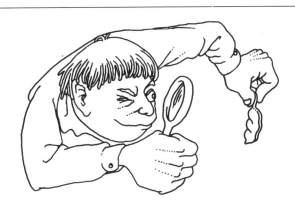

3. Record your observations in three ways:

- Draw your plant and its seed pods on the **Observation Sheet** your teacher gave you.

- Describe your plant in words on the **Observation Sheet**. What happened to the petals and anthers?

- Measure and graph the height of your plant on the plant growth graph.

4. Record your observations at least once a week until Day 35.

Ideas to Explore

1. Dissect, or cut open, one of your seed pods. Use your forceps and toothpicks for tools. What do you see inside?

2. Collect some pods for the class. Leave them in the learning center. Beans and peas come in pods. Can you think of any other pods?

3. Keep track of the progress of one pod. Measure its length carefully each day. Record the measurements. Handle the plant gently so the pod doesn't get pulled off.

Figure 12-2

Different pods

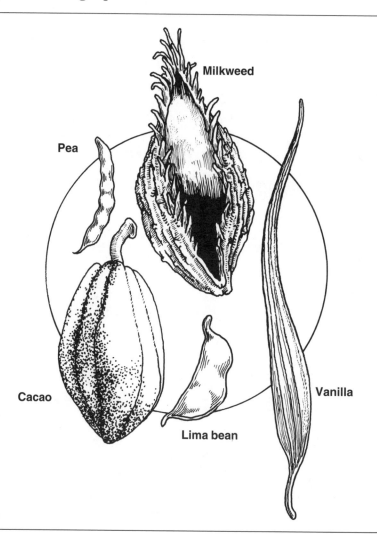

Making a *Brassica* Model

Think and Wonder

You have been observing *Brassica* flowers for several weeks. In fact, you are becoming an expert on these blossoms. One great way to share what you have learned is by making a model. During this lesson, you will learn how.

Materials

For you

Your teacher will pass out materials as needed.

Find Out for Yourself

1. Your teacher will help you get organized into teams. Each team will work together to make a *Brassica* flower.

2. First, have a team planning session. Pick one member of your team to keep a record of your plans. Here are some decisions your team needs to make:

   ■ What should the model look like? If you need to, look at your plant or the drawings you made of your plant to help you decide.

   ■ What materials will you use to build the flower model? Plan to include some recycled materials.

   ■ How will your team divide up the work? Who will do what?

3. Discuss your plans for building the model with your teacher.

4. Your teacher will show you where the materials are. Collect everything you need to build a model.

5. Work with your team to construct the model.

6. Share your model with the class.

Ideas to Explore

Take the time to look at the other flower models your classmates have made. As you look at the other models, think about these things:

■ Does the model have the correct number of petals and anthers?

■ Are the flower parts in the right places?

■ Is the model neat?

■ Is the model attractive?

■ Do you think the team put a lot of effort into making the model?

Figure 13-1

Model of a flower

LESSON 14	# Making a Bee Model

Think and Wonder

You have had experience observing bees and making models of flowers. Today you are going to make a model of a bee. Then, using both models, you can act out how they work together.

Materials

Your teacher will pass out materials as needed.

Find Out for Yourself

1. Your teacher will help you get organized into teams. Each team will make a model of a bee.

2. You and your teammates should begin by planning your bee model together. Here are some decisions your team needs to make:

   ■ What should the bee model look like? Look at the dried bees and the drawings in your notebook to help you decide.

   ■ What materials would be best to use for the bee model? Where can you get these materials? Can some of them be recycled?

   ■ How will your team divide up the work? What job will each person do?

3. Discuss your plans for building the bee model with your teacher.

4. Your teacher will show you where the materials are. Collect everything you need to build a model.

5. Work with your team to construct the model. Your teacher will provide instructions.

6. Share your model with the class.

Ideas to Explore

1. Think about how you would tell the story of pollination to someone who has never heard it before. What new words have you learned that you can use in the story? How could the models help to show what happens?

2. Your teacher will explain how to tell a story taking turns in a "round-robin" style. Some students will get to tell the story of pollination. Others will act it out with the models.

3. Write your own script for this drama that takes place in nature.

Figure 14-1

Model of a bee

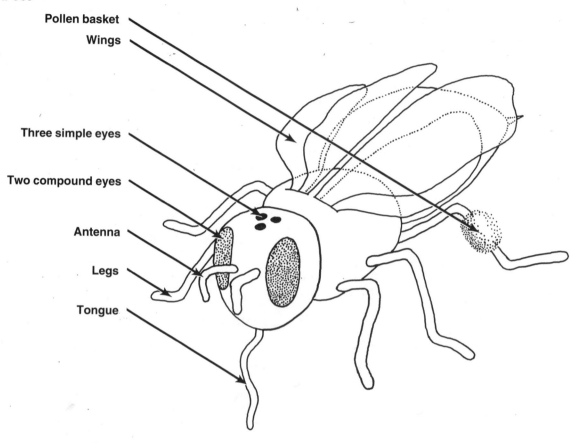

Pollen basket
Wings
Three simple eyes
Two compound eyes
Antenna
Legs
Tongue

| LESSON 15 | **Interpreting Graphs** |

Think and Wonder

You have had a great deal of practice making graphs during this unit. Now you will practice pulling information out of them. You'll be surprised at how much you can learn from graphs. They tell a whole story!

Materials

For you
   1   student notebook

Find Out for Yourself

1.   Look at the bar graph on pg. 44. The graph gives you a picture of how fast Wisconsin Fast Plants™ really are. Use the graph to answer the questions below. Record the answers in your notebook.

   a.   What is the title of the graph?

   b.   How many days does it take for Wisconsin Fast Plants to develop their seeds?

   c.   After Wisconsin Fast Plants, what is the next fastest plant to develop seeds?

   d.   How many days does it take for pea seeds to develop? Notice that the bar stops between the 60- and 65-day marks. Make a good estimate of which day this means.

   e.   Lima beans need 75 days to develop seeds. Corn only needs about 68 days. How many more days does it take for lima beans to develop seeds than corn?

2.   Go over the answers with your teacher. Be sure to ask questions about anything you don't understand.

Figure 15-1

*Graph of
plant life cycles*

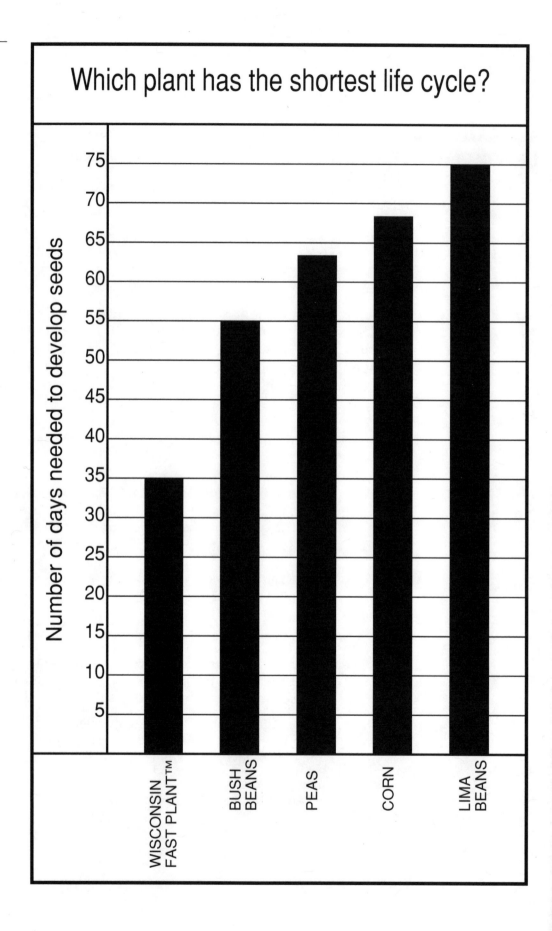

Which plant has the shortest life cycle?

3. Now read about Helen's graph.

Every fourth year, it was Helen's turn to spend the summer at Grandma and Grandpa's farm. Even before she had time to unpack, Grandma would always say "Let's see how much you've grown since the last time you were here." Then the three of them would stroll out to the barn together. Right next to Chester the horse's stall was a smooth plank wall. This was Helen's measuring place. Helen would stand straight with her heels to the wall, and Grandpa would draw a line across the plank to mark her height. Each time they measured, Helen would move over one plank to the right. And she always wrote her age under the measurement. By the time she was 20 years old, that wall looked just like a graph!

Figure 15-2

The plank wall

Figure 15-3

Helen's graph

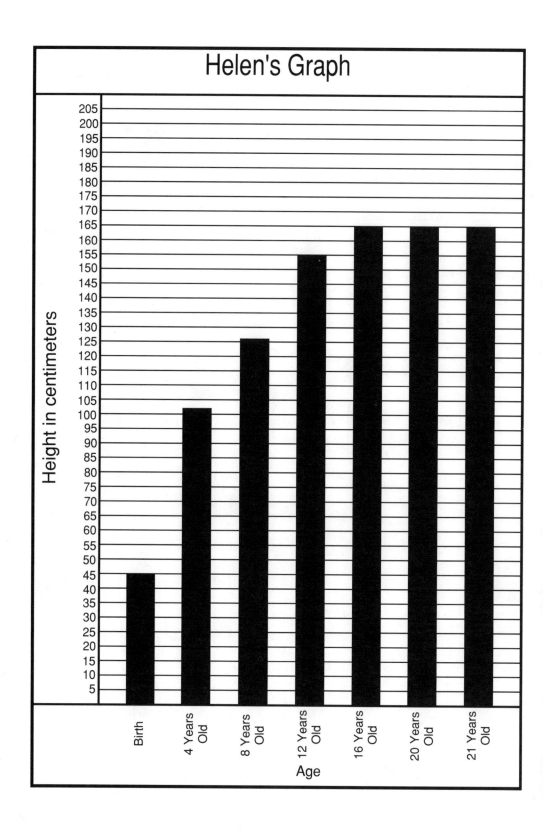

Helen's Graph

Height in centimeters

205
200
195
190
185
180
175
170
165
160
155
150
145
140
135
130
125
120
115
110
105
100
95
90
85
80
75
70
65
60
55
50
45
40
35
30
25
20
15
10
5

Birth | 4 Years Old | 8 Years Old | 12 Years Old | 16 Years Old | 20 Years Old | 21 Years Old

Age

4. Use Helen's graph to answer these questions. Record the answers in your notebook.

   a. Helen was 45 cm long at birth. By the time she was ready to spend her first summer in the country at age 4, she was more than twice that tall. How tall was she at age 4?

   b. Grandpa was big on safety. He insisted that no one could ride Chester alone unless that person was at least 125 cm tall. When Helen was only 4 years old, it seemed like a good rule. But by the time she was 8, Helen was dreaming of riding solo. Did she get her wish that summer when she was 8?

   c. Grandpa had another rule. You had to be at least 150 cm tall to drive the tractor. How old was Helen when she was first allowed to drive the tractor?

   d. At 12, Helen was right in the middle of her adolescent growth spurt. How much taller is she at 12 than she was at 8?

   e. Grandma and Helen stood back to back at the end of her sixteenth summer and discovered that they were exactly the same height—165 cm. Do you think they were still the same height when Helen was 17 years old? Give a good reason for your answer.

5. Go over the answers with your teacher. If there are still some problems, be sure to ask questions so that the teacher can help you.

Ideas to Explore

1. Do you have a special measuring place at home? Try to bring in information about your own growth to put on a graph.

2. It's fun to take a survey. Think of an interesting question, and ask everyone in the class the same question. Record all of the answers. Then put the data on a graph. Here are some sample questions to try.

   ■ What month is your birthday?

   ■ What is your favorite school lunch?

   ■ What color are your eyes?

   ■ How many brothers and sisters do you have?

   ■ What time do you usually go to bed on school nights?

   ■ How many pets do you have?

Harvesting and Threshing the Seed

Think and Wonder

The *Brassica* plant has now completed its life cycle. The plant has died, but something else lives on. Let's learn more about the last stage of a plant's life.

Materials

For you

1 tray
1 envelope to store seeds
1 pair of scissors (optional)
1 paper cup (optional)
1 quad of dried plants
1 student notebook

Find Out for Yourself

1. Pick up your materials.

2. Observe your plant. How has it changed since you took it off the watering system?

   Write down three good words in your notebook to describe the changes.

3. Harvest the pods by snapping them off or cutting them off with scissors. Work over your tray. Record the total number of pods.

4. Thresh the seeds out of the pods by rolling the pods gently between your hands. Work over the tray and try not to lose any seeds. How many seeds did you thresh? Record the total number of seeds in your notebook.

5. Label the envelope with your name and the date. Put your seeds in the envelope for storage.

6. How many more seeds do you have today than you did when you began? Remember, you planted eight seeds. Here's how to find out:

   a. Write down the total number of seeds you have today.

    b.   Subtract the eight seeds you started with.

    c.   The answer is your profit.

7.   Observe the plants you and your classmates set aside after Lesson 4. These plants were not pollinated. What is the result? What does this tell you about the importance of pollination?

8.   You have learned a lot about plants. Do you still have questions? Is there something you are wondering about? Write it down. Be ready to share your thoughts.

9.   What are some of the things you could do to try to find the answer to your questions? Write down your ideas for experiments.

Ideas to Explore

1.   Think about this: How does a farmer make a living? How is his job similar to the plant project?

Figure 16-1

Combine

2.   This machine is called a combine. Find out what the combine does. Do you think it is named correctly?

3.   Use your seeds to do an experiment. Think of a question you still have about plants. What could you do to try to find out the answer? Your teacher will help you plan a good experiment.